Chintz

CERAMICS

Jo Anne P. Welsh

Schiffer Publishing Ltd

4880 Lower Valley Rd. Atglen, PA 19310 USA

Printed in Hong Kong
ISBN: 0-7643-0451-8

Library of Congress Cataloging-in-Publication Data

Welsh, Jo Anne P. (Jo Anne Peterson)
Chintz ceramics / Jo Anne P. Welsh.
p. cm.
Includes bibliographical references and index.
ISBN 0-7643-0451-8
1. Pottery, English--Collectors and collecting--Catalogs.
2. Flowers in art--Catalogs. I. Title.
NK4085.W43   1996
738'.0942--dc20   96-33774
CIP

Published by Schiffer Publishing Ltd.
4880 Lower Valley Road
Atglen, PA 19310
Phone: (610) 593-1777; Fax: (610) 593-2002
E-mail: schifferbk@aol.com
Please write for a free catalog.
This book may be purchased from the publisher.
Please include $3.95 for shipping.
Try your bookstore first.

We are interested in hearing from authors
with book ideas on related subjects.

This book is dedicated to Tom, Matthew, and Elizabeth for their encouragement and their willingness to "stop the car" in search of —— Chintz.——

Acknowledgements

I would like to thank all those who have helped me with this book. In particular I would like to thank Peter Stiltz, the "King of Chintz," for his knowledge and friendship throughout this project. I also want to thank Joy Humphreys for her help in finding chintz patterns in England. Special thanks go to the following people who have helped so much: Julie Ainsworth, Jody Baldwin, Dennis Boyd, Candyce Brosz, Bernadene Burdick, Bob and Judy Coleman, Chris Davenport, Angie Davis, Matt Ellenberg, Jane Fehrenbacher, Penny Ferguson, Harry "China Finders", Peter Griffin, Jeanette Halls, Mary Harris, Mark and Laurie Hedtler, Taylor Hoag, Corey Hobbins, Helena Hofer, Noel Izon, Geoffrey Jackson, Hinda Jaffrey, Bob and Doreen Johnson, Lem Lamont, Joan Lease, Joe Mangiafico, Marion Marquis, Bill Miller, Muriel Miller, David Nicklin, Jacqulyn Peterson, Nels Peterson, LaVonn Rogers, Brenda and Richard Bennett Smith, Kit Tacie, Stefani and Gordon Tosto, June Tracy, Tom Wachs, Susan Walker, Denise Walters, Taylor Wells, Tony Whiteford, Diana Williams, Jane Workman, Gwen Zellars.

Contents

Introduction

Chintz ceramics has its origins in a city called Stoke-on-Trent in England. Stoke-on-Trent was formed in 1910 from the surrounding towns of Burslem, Fenton, Hanley, Longton, Stoke, and Tunstall. The abundance of clay and coal in the area provided the raw materials to produce many of the finest ceramics in the world.

The earliest ceramics with chintz decoration date back to the late 1800s when the transfer printing process was popular. Many of the manufacturers were using engravers who would engrave the copper plates that would create the image on tissue paper. The transferer would transfer the design from the tissue paper to the ceramic piece. The transfer was rubbed down with a stiff brush to ensure consistent contact. The paper was then washed off with a sponge, thus leaving the design on the piece. Prior to the mid-1860s, the design left on the piece was all one color, so that other colors had to be painted by hand. In the case of the early chintz decoration, only the outline was showing so all the flowers had to be painted to resemble their natural colors and beauty.

A page from the Grimwade Ltd. catalog, c. 1920. Notice the many shapes manufactured.

During the mid-1860s a new process was discovered that would produce colored designs by a means of lithographic printing. It was cheaper to produce and the colors were true to their natural color. In 1895, one of the men associated with the production of duplex paper used for lithographs was Leonard Grimwade of Grimwades, Ltd. He and others developed a duplex paper strong enough to go through the printing process but having a thin layer on top that would be detached and applied to the curved surfaces of the ceramic. Chintz patterns produced from 1928 to the present are applied by the lithograph process.

The following is an interview with Vera Hopkinson, from Stoke-on-Trent, who worked in the pottery industry for fifty-four years.

Jo Anne: Vera, would you please tell me how you would decorate a piece of chintz?

Vera: Well, you had varnish and a soft brush and you painted the piece that you were going to lithograph. You left it on one side until it was tacky. Then, the chintz was on big sheets and you cut it to fit whatever you were doing. Then you put it on and pressed it all down into the grooves. You rubbed it on with a wet sponge. Then you got a soapy sponge and took the lining off it. Of course, there was a backing on the litho, and that came off. You washed it with a rag.

Jo Anne: After you took the top piece off with a sponge, did you cut away the excess?

Vera: Oh yes. See, you cut the litho to fit whatever you were doing. Well, you wouldn't get it perfect. You would have to trim around it with scissors to make it fit properly.

Jo Anne: When you were making a piece, if the transfer wasn't put on properly, would it be broken and thrown away?

Vera: Well, you could wash it off with warm water. The lacquer would wash off with warm water.

Jo Anne: So, you could start again?

Vera: Oh, yes, start again.

Jo Anne: Which were the hardest pieces to put the transfers on?

Vera: The veg dishes, the big veg dishes. Inside cups—those were quite hard.

Jo Anne: Vera, what positions did you hold during your fifty-four years working in the potteries?

Vera: Well, I was a lithographer at first. Of course I progressed on and was over the girls. I was a supervisor. I used to do the wages and everything, show them what to do.

Jo Anne: When you were a lithographer, were the lithographers paid more than the gilders?

Vera: Oh, no, we were all piecework. You were paid for what you did.

Jo Anne: Everybody was paid piecework?

Vera: Yes.

Jo Anne: Thank you very much.

Royal Winton produced the most chintz patterns and was considered the industry leader. However, there were several other manufacturers that produced chintz. I have seen examples of the same pattern on both earthenware and china. For example, pieces have been found of "Blue Pansy" on Lord Nelson, Shelley, H&K Tunstall, and Salisbury. "Rose DuBarry," a pattern produced by Royal Winton, also shows up on Shelley as "Briar Rose" and also on Crown Clarence. This explains that lithograph patterns were produced by the leading manufacturers and also by smaller companies who sold them as open stock.

Chapter 1
Royal Winton

- 1886-Present
- Earthenware
- Stoke

Grimwade Brothers was founded in 1885 by Leonard, Edward, and Sydney Grimwade in Stoke-on-Trent. In 1892, Winton Pottery was built. As the brothers became more successful, they acquired Stoke Pottery and Winton Pottery Co., Ltd., in 1900, and changed the company name to Grimwades, Ltd. In 1906 they acquired the Upper Hanley Pottery Co., Ltd., and the Atlas China Co. In 1907 they bought Heron Cross Pottery. By 1913 the company employed about 1,500 people, which made it one of the largest pottery firms in the area. In 1930, following Royal patronage from King George V and Queen Mary, the prefix "Royal" was added.

The first lithograph chintz produced by Royal Winton was in 1928 and named "Marguerite." According to Muriel Miller, "Leonard Grimwade's younger daughter, Ruth, was told that the design was taken from a cushion cover being embroidered by her mother.[1]

The November 1, 1929, issue of "Pottery Gazette and Glass Trade Review" reveals that "'Marguerite Chintz,' a treatment embodying a very pleasing ground tint in natural colours, and a theme expressive of the charm of the countryside, the shapes being new and unquestionably appealing." A photo appears showing the range of pieces that can be purchased and the trade magazine recommends that these pieces would be "eminently suitable for the Christmas trade."[2]

The September 1, 1931 issue of "The Pottery Gazette and Glass Trade Review" includes an ad from the Grimwades, Ltd., company introducing "Delphinium Chintz" which states "an attractive adaptation of a popular English summer flower."[3]

Marguerite, Plate, 6.5", Mark 1, $50-75.

Delphinium, Saucer, 5.5", Mark 1.

Previous Page: Winton House (vacant). Chintz was made here until 1963.

[1] Miller, Muriel. *Antique Collecting*, Vol. 27, No. 2, June 1992, p.32.
[2] *Pottery Gazette and Glass Trade Review*, November 1, 1929, p.1745.
[3] *Pottery Gazette and Glass Trade Review*, September 1, 1931.

In the July 1932 issue of "The Pottery Gazette and Glass Trade Review," Grimwades, Ltd. is said to "have always applied themselves very assiduously to supply pottery dealers whose interests are associated with the masses and middle classes. Chintzes, which have long been a popular line in Winton ware, are still favored. The trade will readily recall the old 'Marguerite Chintz' was a tremendous success. This has now been succeeded by a pattern which has been christened 'Summertime.' It is sort of fantasia, compounded of roses, daisies, violets, harebells, and similar summer-time flowers."[4]

During the next thirty years, Royal Winton introduced over fifty more chintz patterns.

Pottery Gazette & Glass Trade Review, 1947. Advertisement for Royal Winton Chintz. Chintz was exported to Australia, U.S.A., Canada, South Africa, and New Zealand.

Then on October 30, 1963, Royal Winton was acquired by Howard Pottery Co., Ltd., and the production of chintz was ended. They moved to Norfolk Street where Royal Winton today is a successful company producing giftware, tableware, and kitchenware sold throughout the world.

[4] *Pottery Gazette and Glass Trade Review,* July 1, 1932, p.865.

Summertime,
Plate, 8", Mark 4.
$75-100

Pottery Gazette & Glass Trade Review, April 1952. Notice the chintz fabric for the window treatment.

Pottery Gazette & Glass Trade Review, January 1950. Chintz is advertised as "the ware with appeal."

Pottery Gazette & Glass Trade Review, 1948. Royal Winton is still "famous for chintz."

Brass plaque commemorating the visit of the Prince of Wales to Royal Winton in November 1988.

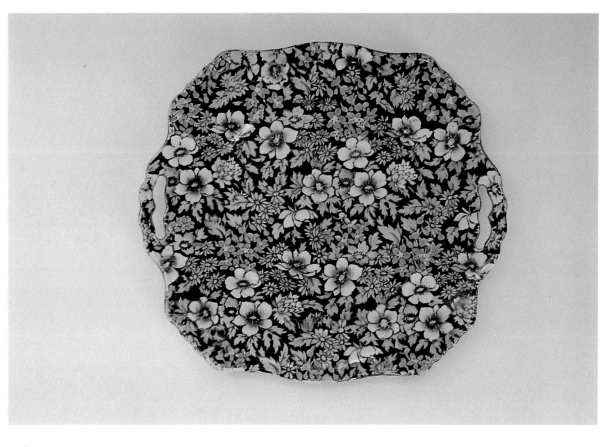

Anemone, Cake Plate, 9.5", Hand Painted, Mark 3, $125-150.

During my recent visit to Stoke-on-Trent I had the pleasure of meeting Peter Griffin, the Managing Director of Royal Winton. I asked Mr. Griffin why Royal Winton stopped making chintz.

He responded "In the '60s in this country and in the industry it was a time when cost-effectiveness started to take over and shapes had to be made to be mass produced and decorations had to be capable of being applied very cheaply. So, anything that was labor intensive, and applying chintz decorations properly was very labor intensive, they started to be cut."

Patterns

Balmoral, Saucer, 5.5", Mark 9.

Anemone, Plate, 8.5", Hand Painted, Mark 3, $100-125.

Beeston, Cream, 3", Mark 4, $75-100.

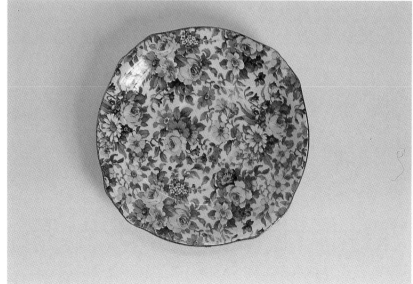

Bedale, Saucer, 5.5", Mark 2.

Cheadle, Saucer, 5.5", Mark 9.

Clevedon, Sugar Bowl, 3.5", Mark 4, $75-100.

Chelsea, Saucer, 5", Mark 7.

Clyde, Small Jug, 4.5", Mark 4, $125-150

Cotswold, Saucer, 5.5", Mark 7.

Cranstone, Cream, 3", Mark 5, $75-100.

Crocus, White, Plate, 5", Mark 9, $50-75.

Crocus pattern close-up.

Dorset, Plate, 6.75", Mark 6, $50-75.

Crocus, Black, Pin Dish, 4.25", Mark 4, $50-75. (Also named Triumph)

Cromer, Sweet Dish, 5.25" X 4.75", Mark 4, $50-75.

Delphinium, Saucer, 5.5", Mark 1.

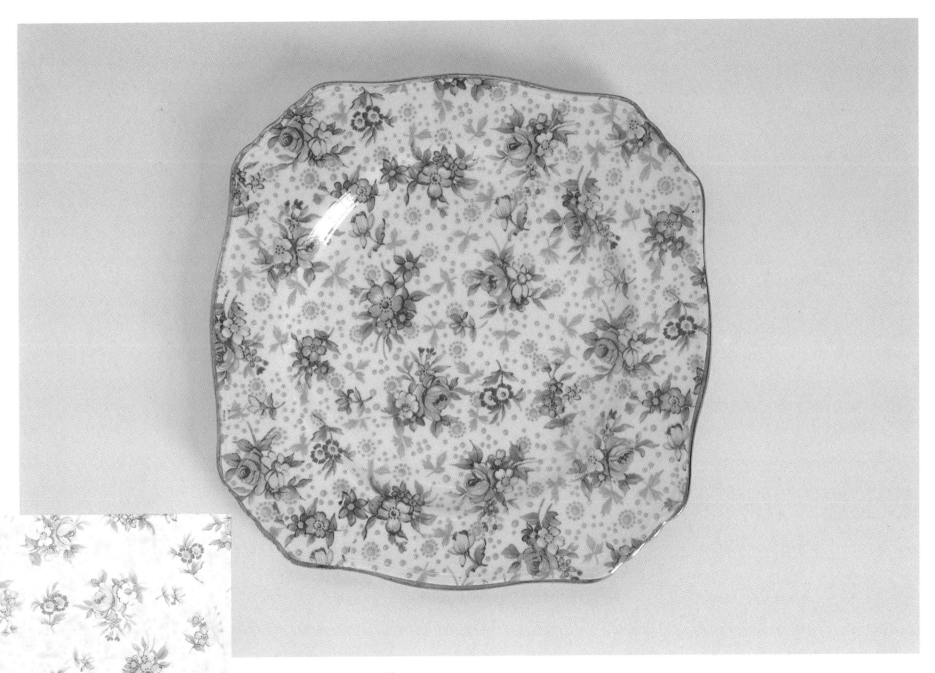

Eleanor, Plate, 6", Mark 9, $50-75.

Eleanor pattern close-up.

Estelle, Plate, 8", Mark 6, $75-100.

Esther, Saucer, 4.5", Mark 8.

Evesham, Saucer, 5.5", Mark 7.

English Rose, Plate, 5", Mark 9, $50-75.

Fireglow, White, Plate, 5", Mark 4, $50-75.

Fireglow, Black, Pin Dish, 4.25", Mark 9, $50-75.

Floral Feast, Sweet Dish, 5" X 5", Mark 1, $50-75.

Florence, Saucer, 5.5", Mark 6.

Hazel, Plate, 6", Mark 4, $50-75.

Hazel pattern close-up.

Joyce Lynn, Saucer, 5.5", Mark 4.

Julia, Saucer, 5.5", Mark 4.

June Festival, Saucer, 5.5", Mark 6.

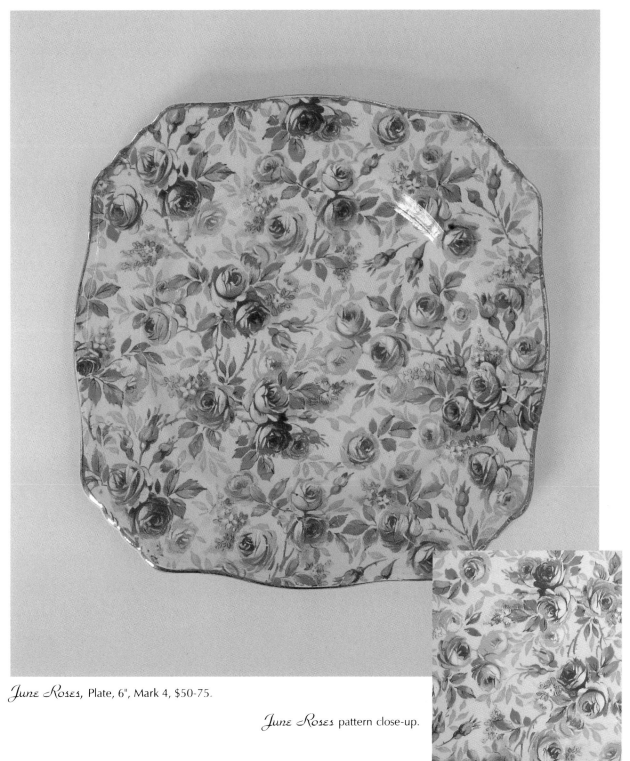

June Roses, Plate, 6", Mark 4, $50-75.

June Roses pattern close-up.

Kinver, Tray, 12", Mark 1, $150-175.

Majestic, Cream, 2.5", Mark 4, $75-100.

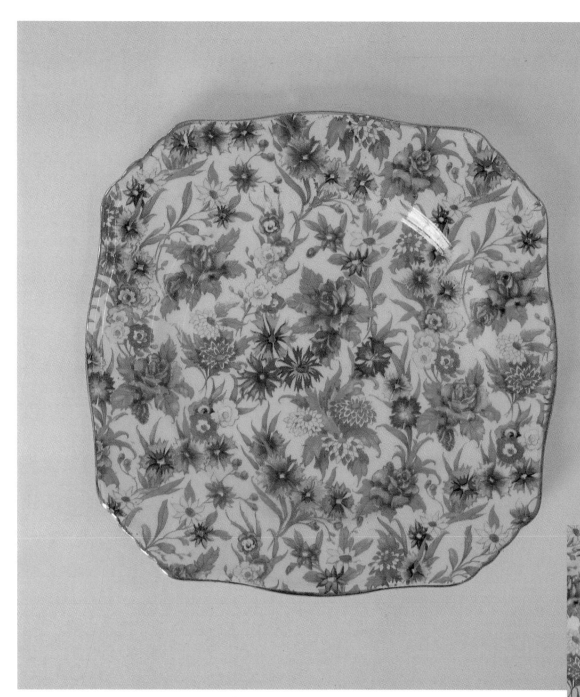

Kew, Plate, 6", Mark 4, $50-75.

Kew pattern close-up.

Marion, Plate, 7", Mark 9, $75-100.

Marion pattern close-up.

May Festival, Cream, 2.5", Mark 6, $75-100.

Mayfair, Saucer, 6.25", Mark 7.

Morning Glory, Plate, 7", Mark 6, $50-75.

Nantwich, Plate, 6", Mark 4, $50-75.

Old Cottage, Tray, 8", Mark 4, $100-150.

Old Cottage pattern close-up.

Orient, Solitaire Tray, 9", Mark 8, $75-100.

Pelham, Salad Bowl, 8" diameter, Unmarked, $125-150.

Peony, Creamer, 3", Mark 6, $75-100.

Paisley, Salt Shaker, 2.5", Mark 9, $25-35.

Queen Anne, Plate, 7.75", Mark 4, $75-100.

Richmond, Honey Pot, 2.5", Mark 4, $50-75.

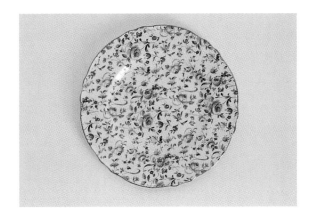

Rose DuBarry, Plate, 7", Mark 4, $75-100.

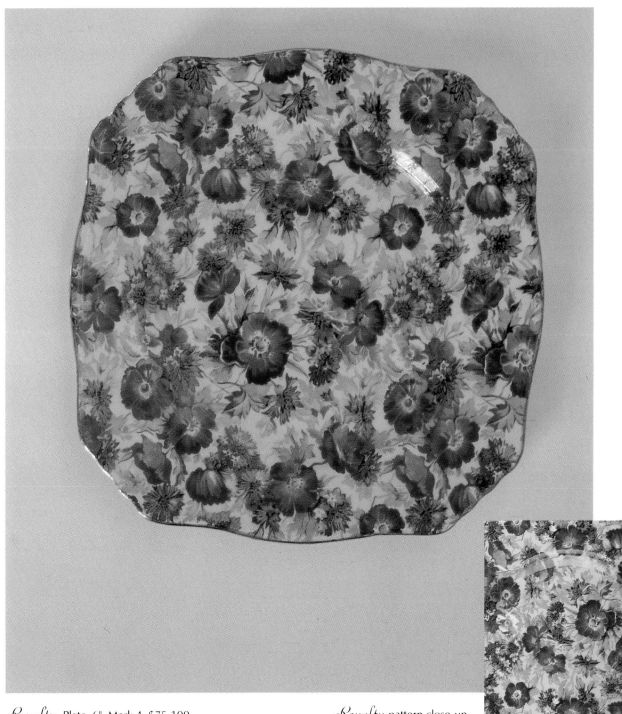

Royalty, Plate, 6", Mark 4, $75-100.

Royalty pattern close-up.

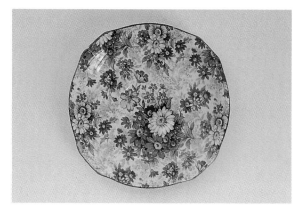

Rutland, Saucer, 5.5", Mark 1.

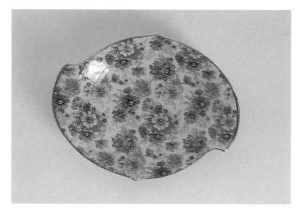

Shrewsbury, Sweet Dish, 7.25" X 5.5", Mark 6, $75-100.

Somerset, Plate, 8", Mark 1, $100-150.

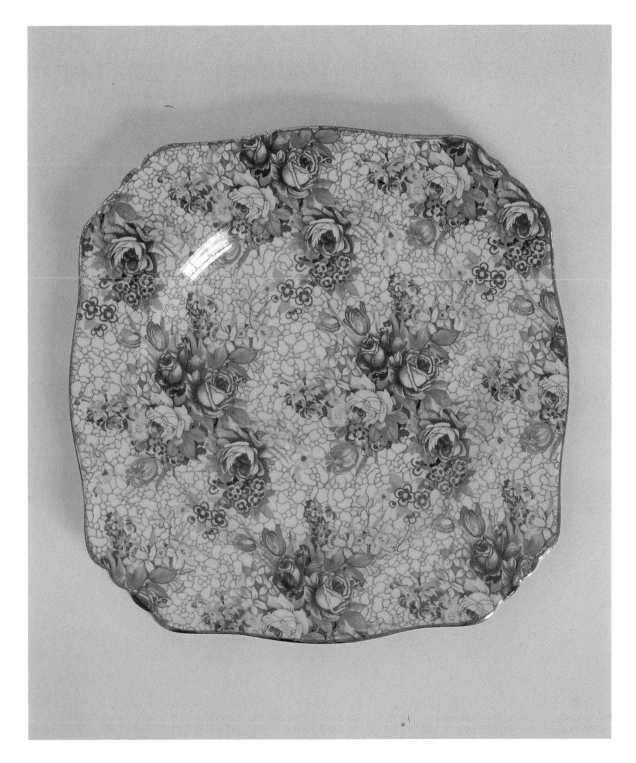

Spring pattern close-up.

Spring, Plate, 6", Mark 4, $50-75.

Spring Glory, Cream, 2.5", Mark 6, $75-100.

Springtime, Plate, 7", Mark 1, $75-100.

Springtime pattern close-up.

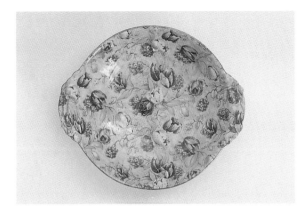

Stratford, Sweet Dish, 5.5" X 4.5", Mark 9, $100-125.

Summertime, Bowl, 7.5", Mark 1, $50-75.

Sunshine, Saucer, 5.5", Mark 4.

Sweet Nancy, Cream, 3", Mark 4, $75-100.

Victorian, Plate, 7.75", Mark 4, $75-100.

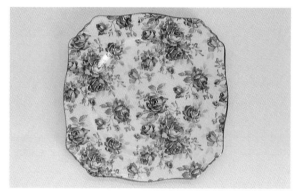

Victorian Rose, Plate, 7", Mark 9, $75-100.

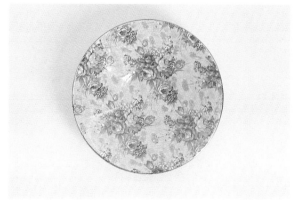

Welbeck, Saucer, 5.75", Mark 4.

Sweet Pea, cream, 2.75" high,
Ascot Shape, Mark 4, $75-100.

Wild Flowers, Sugar, 3", Mark 4, $75-100.

Winifred, Tray, 8" X 5", Mark 6, $100-125.

No Name, Cake Plate, 2" high X 8" diameter, Mark 4, $100-125.

No Name, Cream, 2.5" high, Mark 1, $50-75.

No Name, Cream, 3" high, Mark 1, $50-75.

Shapes

Esther, Demi Cup, 2.25" high, Mark 8.

Old Cottage, Cup, 2.25" high, Mark 4.

Spring, Cup, 2.75" high, Mark 4.

English Rose, Cup, 2.75" high, Mark 7.

Chelsea, Demi Cup, 2.5" high, Mark 7.

Old Cottage, Cup, 3" high, Mark 4.

Old Cottage, Demi Cup, 2.25" high, Mark 4.

June Festival, Cup, 3" high, Mark 6.

Sunshine, Cup, 3" high, Mark 4.

Julia, Cup, 2.75" high, Mark 4.

Rose DuBarry, Cup and Saucer, 2.75" high X 5.5" diameter, Mark 4, $75-100. Mini Cup and Saucer (Rosina), 1" high X 1" diameter, $100-150.

Summertime pattern close-up.

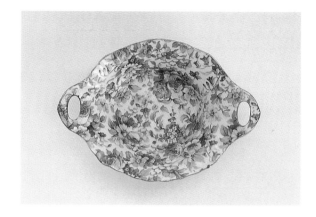

Summertime, Sweet Dish, 4", Mark 4, $75-100.

Summertime, Sugar, 1.75" high X 3.25" diameter, Mark 1. Cream, 2.25" high X 3" diameter, Mark 1, $150-175.

Summertime, Sugar, 2.25" high X 3.75" diameter, Mark 4. Creamer, 4.5" high, Mark 7, $150-175.

Beeston, Sugar Bowl, 2.75" high X 4" diameter, Mark 4, $75-100.

June Festival, Coffee Pot (4 cup), 8.5" high, Mark 6, $400-600.

Summertime, Teapot (4 cup), 6.75" high X 4.5" diameter, Mark 4, $400-600.

Summertime, Teapot (3 cup), 5.75" high X 3.5" diameter, Mark 7, $300-600.

Summertime, Teapot (5 cup), 6" high, Mark 4, $500-800.

Summertime, Teapot (4 cup), 5" high, Mark 4, $400-600.

Floral Feast, Teapot (2 cup), Norman Shape, 5" high, Mark 4, $400-600.

Floral Feast, Teapot (1 cup), 4.5" high, Mark 1, $100-200.

English Rose, Stacking Teapot (1 cup), 6" high, Mark 9, $1000-1200.

Summertime, Hot Water Pot (2 cup), 5.5" high, Mark 1, $200-400.

Queen Anne, Sweet Dish, 5", Mark 9, $50-75.

Queen Anne, Bell, 5", Mark 4, $100-200.
(Very rare)

Julia, Cream, 3" high, Mark 4, $75-100.

English Rose, Jug, Globe Shape, 4.25" high, Mark 9, $350-400.

Old Cottage, Jug, 4" high, Mark 9, $200-250.

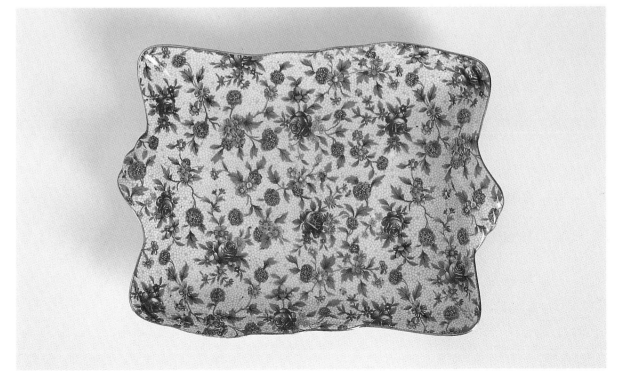

Old Cottage, Tray, 9", Mark 4, $100-125.

Sweet Pea, Cream, 2.75" high, Ascot Shape, Mark 4, $75-100.

Old Cottage, Cream, 2.5" high, Ascot Shape, Mark 4, $75-100.

Floral Feast, Cream, 2.75" high, Norman Shape, Mark 4, $75-100.

Summertime, Cream, 2.5" high, Mark 1, $75-100.

Welbeck, Cream, 3.5" high, Mark 4, $75-100.

Old Cottage, Cream, 3" high, Mark 4, $75-100.

Summertime, Jug, 5" high, Globe Shape, Mark 4, $200-400.

Rutland, Bowl, 2" high X 4" diameter, Mark 1, $50-100.

Mayfair, Vase, 4" high, Mark 4, $100-150.

Old Cottage, Mustard Pot, 2.5" high,
Mark 4, $100-150.

Summertime, Vase, 5" high, Mark 4, $100-150.

Kinver, Honey Pot, 3.5" high, Mark 4, $200-250.

Kew, Cruet Set (Salt, Pepper, Mustard Pot), 2.5" high, Mark 9, $150-200.

Sunshine, Vase, 3.5" high, Mark 4, $100-125.

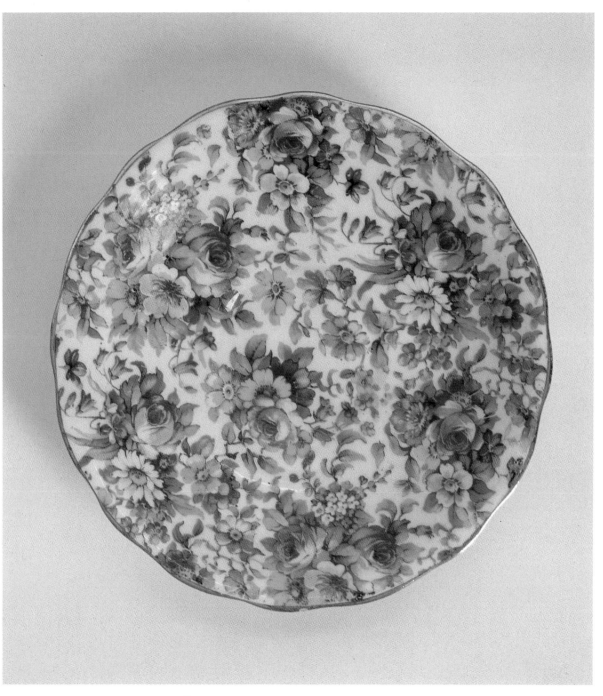

Summertime, Saucer, 5.5", Atlas China Mark 5.

Summertime, Mustard Pot, 1.5" high, $50-75.

Summertime, Jam Pot, 4" high, Mark 4,
Under Plate, 4.5" X 4.5", $100-150.

Marion, Mustard Pot, 3.5" high, Mark 2, $75-100.

Kew, Toast Rack, 2.5" high X 7" diameter,
Mark 4, $200-250.

Florence, Candy Box, 8", Mark 6, $200-300.

Summertime, Cheese Dish, 3" high X 5.5" wide, Mark 4, $250-300.

Summertime, Cheese Dish, 2.25" high X 4" wide, Mark 4, $250-300.

Old Cottage, Covered Butter Dish, 2.5" high X 5.5" wide, Mark 4, $250-300.

Marion, Basket, 5" high X 5" long, Mark 9, $200-300.
(Very rare)

Summertime, Salt and Pepper, 2" high, $100-150.

Summertime, Salt and Pepper, 2.5" high, $100-150.

Summertime, Salt and Pepper on Tray, 3" high X 6" long, Mark 4, $150-200.

Old Cottage, Sugar Bowl, 2.5" high X 4.75" diameter, Mark 9, $75-100.

Floral Feast, Covered Sugar, 4" high X 4.5" diameter, Mark 1, $100-150.

Summertime, Mayonnaise Bowl, 2.5" high X 4.5" diameter, Mark 4, $200-250.

Kew, Open Sugar, 2" high X 3.5" diameter, Mark 4, $75-100.

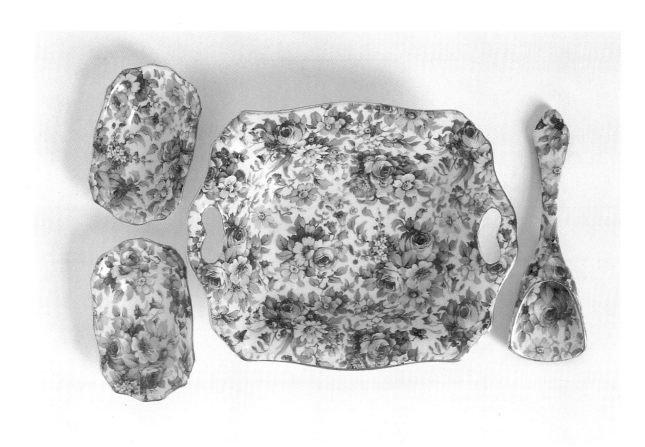

Summertime, Nut Dish, 6.5" X 5", Scoop, 5" long, and 2 Individual Nut Dishes, 3.25" X 2", Mark 4, $350-400.

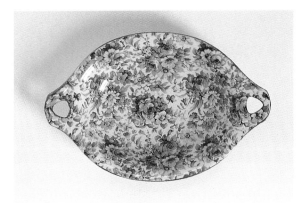

Summertime, Bowl, 8.5" long X 5.5" wide,
Mark 4, $50-75.

Old Cottage, Butter Pat, 3.25" X 3.25",
Mark 4, $30-50.

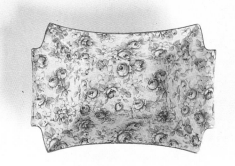

English Rose, Sweet Dish, 6" X 3.5",
Mark 4, $75-100.

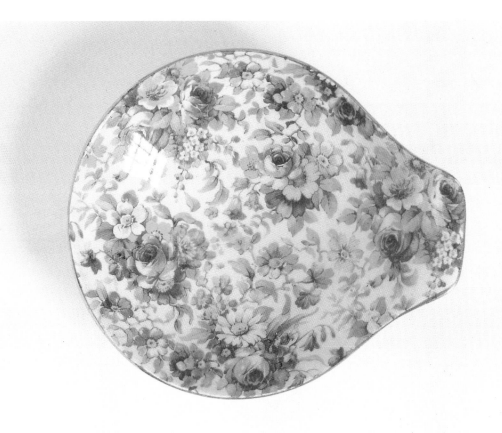

Summertime, Sweet Dish, 5.25" X 4.5", Mark 4, $75-100.

Summertime, Shell Dish, 5" X 4.25", Mark 4, $50-75.

Julia, Ashtray, 3.5" X 2.75", Mark 4, $50-60.

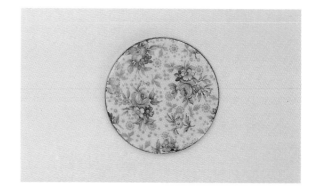

Summertime, Ashtray, 4" X 4", Mark 4, $50-75.

Eleanor, Coaster, 2.75" diameter, Mark 4, $50-75.

Rose DuBarry, Breakfast Set: Teapot, Toast Rack, Cream, Sugar, Cup and Saucer, Mark 4, $600-800.

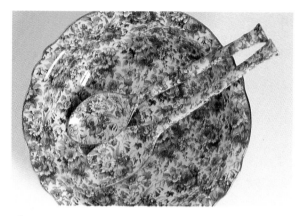

Summertime, Salad Bowl, 9.5" diameter, Fork and Spoon, Mark 9, $300-350.

Summertime, Canoe Dish, 11" X 4.75", Mark 4, $200-250.

Eleanor, Covered Box, 1.5" X 5.5" X 3.5", Mark 9, $175-200.

Summertime, Lamp Base, 9" X 6", Mark 4, $700-900.
(Very rare)

Old Cottage, Trivet, 7" X 7", Mark 4, $100-150.

Summertime, Round Dinner Plate, 10", Mark 4, $125-150.

Summertime, Square Dinner Plate, 9.5", Mark 4, $125-150.

Marion, Bowl (left), 1.5" high X 6.5" diameter, Mark 9, $55-75.
Cotswold, Bowl (right), 1.5" high X 6.5" diameter, Mark 4, $55-75.

Summertime, Cream Soup, 2.25" high X 3.5" diameter, Mark 4, $100-125.

Summertime, Cream Soup, 2" high X 5" diameter, Plate, 5.5" diameter, Mark 4, $125-150.

Sweet Pea, Bowl, 2.5" high X 6.5" diameter, Mark 4, $55-75.
Summertime, Bowl, 2" high X 6.25" diameter, Mark 4, $55-75.

Summertime, Gravy/Stand, 3" high X 7" long, Mark 4, $200-250.

Summertime, Mint Sauce/Stand, 2" high X 5" long, Mark 4, $150-200.

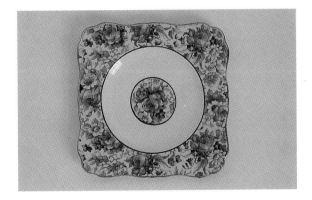

Summertime, Plate, 6", Mark 1, $75-100.

Nantwich, Bowl, 10", Mark 4, $150-200.

Marion, Wall Pocket, 8.5" X 5", Mark 4, $700-900.
(Very rare)

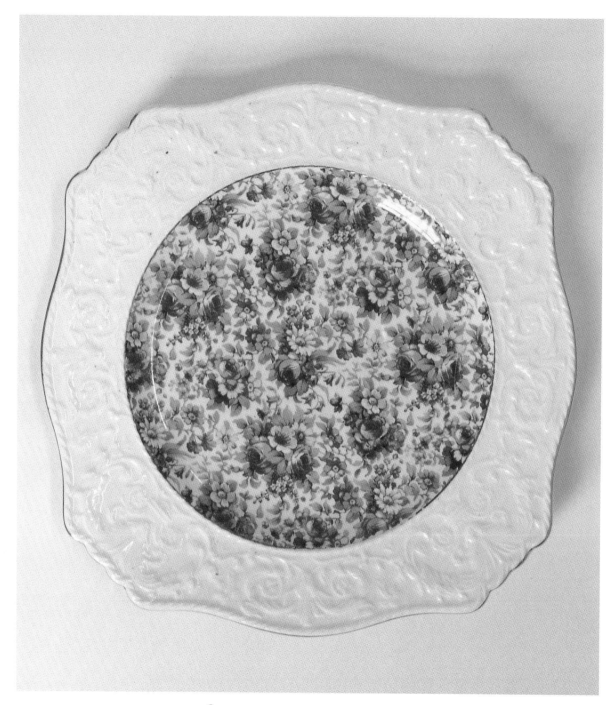

Summertime, Plate, 12", Mark 4, $150-200.

Summertime, Cake Plate, 11", Mark 4, $150-200.

Summertime, Oval Platter, 13" X 10", Mark 4, $200-250.

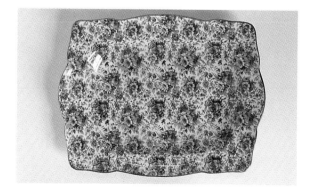

Summertime, Rectangular Platter, 14" X 10", Mark 9, $300-350.

Summertime, 6-Compartment Dish, 12" X 10.75", Mark 4, $250-300.

Summertime, 4-Compartment Dish, 12" X 6", Mark 4, $200-250.

Summertime, 5-Compartment Dish, 11" diameter, Mark 4, $250-300.

Summertime, Tea Tile, 5.75" X 5.75", Mark 9, $100-125.

Summertime, Open Vegetable, 9.25" X 7", Mark 4, $150-200.

Summertime, Bowl, 1.25" high X 8.25", Mark 4, $55-75.

Summertime, Egg Cups, Single 2.5", Double 3.5", Mark 4, $75-100.

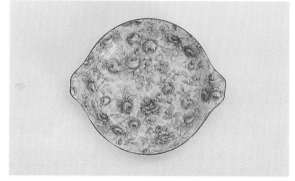

English Rose, Dish, 4.5" X 4", Mark 4, $75-100.

Sweet Pea, Egg Set, 6", Mark 4, $200-300.

Marguerite, Egg Set and Salt and Pepper, 4", Mark 1, $150-200.

Summertime, Egg Set: Tray with Salt and Pepper, 6", Mark 4, $200-300.

Marks

Mark 1, c. 1930+

Mark 2, c. 1930+

Mark 3, c. 1934-1950

Mark 4, c. 1934-1950

Mark 5, c. 1934-1939

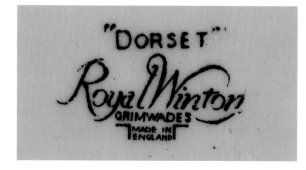

Mark 6, c. 1951+

Mark 7, c. 1951+

Mark 8, C. 1951+

Mark 9, c. 1951+

Chapter 2
James Kent

- 1897-Present
- China and Earthenware
- Longton

In 1897, the firm began as James Kent, Ltd., in Longton using the trade name Old Foley. In 1986, the company was purchased by Fleshpots, Ltd. and renamed James Kent Limited using trade names James Kent, Old Foley, Fleshpots, and Foley. During this period DuBarry was reintroduced as giftware. See catalog. In 1989, the company was purchased by M.R. Hadida and is currently in business today.

Author's Note—Recent 1995 auction item in Litchfield included twelve place settings of James Kent "DuBarry" said to have been given as a wedding present in 1942 to an employee of James Kent. She had selected "DuBarry" as her favorite pattern, even though it was then being produced only for the American market.

August 1952 Advertisement for "*Rosalynde*," Old Foley Ware exported to Canada, Australia, New Zealand, British West Indies, South Africa, Norway, Belgium, and Ireland.

Previous Page: James Kent Factory (still in use), Hadida, Longton, Stoke-on-Trent.

Apple Blossom, Plate, 8", Mark 1, $75-100.

Apple Blossom pattern close-up.

Crazy Paving, Cup, 3" high, Mark 5.

DuBarry, Plate, 8", Mark 2, $75-100.

DuBarry pattern close-up.

Chelsea Rose, Open Sugar, 2" high X 3" diameter, Mark 4, $75-100.

Florita, Regal Tray, 12", Mark 4, $200-250.

Hydrangea, Saucer, 5.5", Mark 3.

Mille Fleurs, Cream, 2.75" High, Mark 2, $75-100.

Hydrangea, Tray, 8", Mark 4, $100-125.

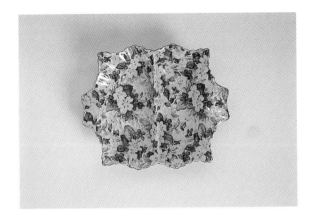

Primula, Divided Dish, 7" X 5.5", Mark 1, $100-150.

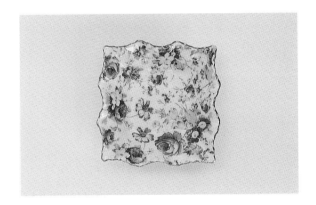

Rapture, Nut Dish, 3" X 3", Mark 1, $25-50.

Rosalynde, Plate, 6.5", Mark 5, $75-100.

Rosalynde pattern close-up.

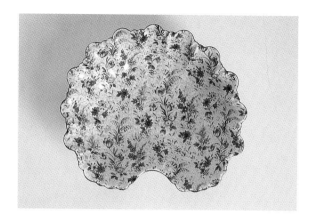

Tapestry, Saucer, 4", Mark 6.

Silverdale, Crescent Bowl, 9", Mark 1, $75-100.

No Pattern Name, Twin Tray, 10" X 6", Mark 2, $100-125.

Primula, Sugar, 2.5" high X 2.25" diameter, and Cream, 2.5" high X 2.25" diameter, Mark 1, $200-250.

Shapes

DuBarry, Cream, 2" high X 2" diameter, and Mini Sugar, 1.25" high X 2" diameter, Mark 6, $150-200.

Apple Blossom, Cream, 2.5" high X 2.75" diameter, and Sugar, 2.25" high X 3" diameter, Mark 1, $200-250.

DuBarry, Sugar, 2" high X 2.75" diameter, and Cream, 2.5" high X 2" diameter, Mark 3, $200-250.

Rosalynde, Open Sugar, 2" high X 3" diameter, Mark 3, $75-100.

DuBarry, Open Sugar, 2.25" high X 2.75" diameter, Mark 3, $75-100.

DuBarry, Octagon Open Sugar, 2.5" high X 3" diameter, Mark 3, $75-100.

Florita, Cream, 2" high X 2" diameter, Mark 6, $75-100.

Rosalynde, Cream, 3.5" high, X 2.75" diameter, Mark 3, $75-100.

DuBarry, Pepper Pot, 2" high, $75-100.

DuBarry, Cream, 2.5" high X 4" long, Mark 6, $75-100.

DuBarry, Toast Rack, 2.5" high X 6" long, Mark 3, $150-200.

DuBarry, Bowl, 2.75" high X 5" diameter, Mark 2, $125-150.

Apple Blossom, Twin Tray, 10" X 6", Mark 1, $200-250.

Apple Blossom, Rectangular Dish, 7.5" X 5", Mark 1, $100-125.

Mille Fleurs, Teapot (4 cup), 6.5" high, Mark 7, $500-700.

DuBarry, TV Set, 8.5" X 5", Demi Cup, 2.25" high, Mark 6, $125-150.

DuBarry, Sandwich Tray, 12", Mark 6, $200-225.

DuBarry, Sweet Dish, 5" X 5", Mark 3, $75-100.

DuBarry, Nut Dish, 3" X 3", Mark 4, $25-45.

Hydrangea, Nut Dish, 5" X 2.75", Mark 1, $50-75.

Hydrangea, Nut Dish, 3.33" X 3", Mark 4, $50-75.

Apple Blossom, Oval Shell, 6", Mark 1, $100-150.

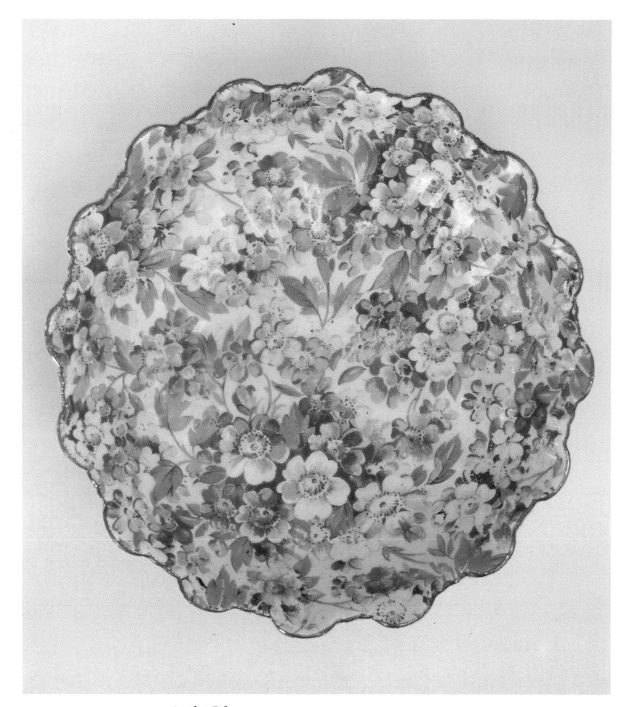

Apple Blossom, Sweet Dish, 7" X 5", Mark 1, $100-150.

DuBarry, Cup, 3" high X 3.25" diameter, Mark 3.

Apple Blossom, Cup, 2.5" high X 3.5" diameter, Mark 1.

Apple Blossom, Demi Cup, 2.25" high X 3" diameter, Mark 1.

Rosalynde, Demi Cup, 2.25" high X 2" diameter, Mark 6.

Rosalynde, Honey Pot with Attached Plate, 3.5" high X 3.75" diameter, Mark 3, $100-150.

Apple Blossom, Round Shell, 7", Mark 1, $75-100.

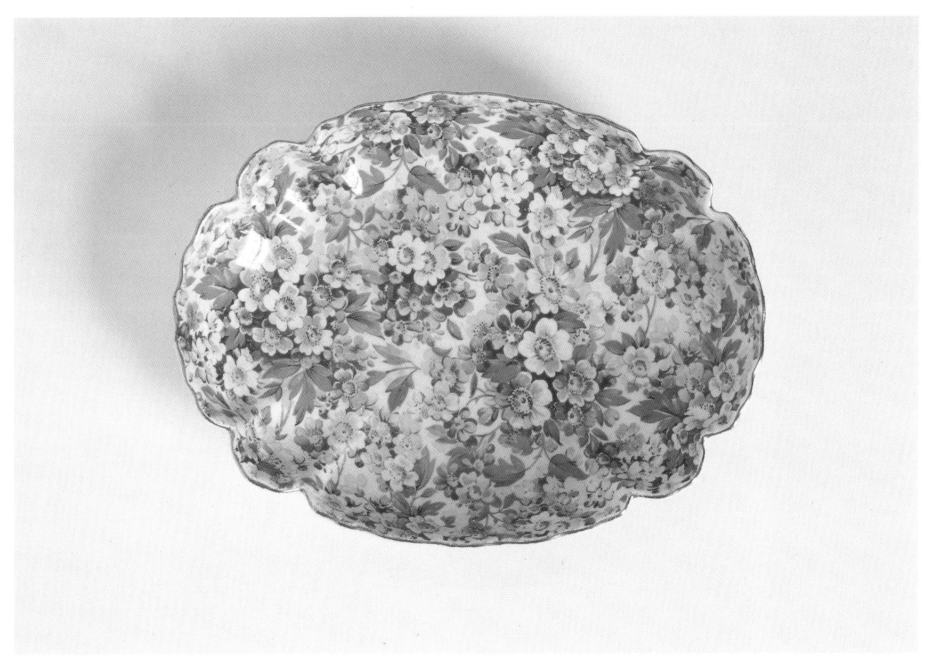

Apple Blossom, Round Dish, 7", Mark 1, $75-100.

Earthenware Cream with *DuBarry* lithograph applied to handle.

DuBarry lithograph before being applied to earthenware.

DuBarry, Cream, Lithograph applied all over piece before final firing.

DuBarry, Creams. Left, before firing. Right, after firing.

DuBarry, Beaker, 4" high, 1995.

DuBarry, Plate, 8", Mark 3.

DuBarry, Saucer, 5.5", 1995.

"Du Barry" PATTERN

by

THE OLD FOLEY POTTERY

IN FINEST SEMI-PORCELAIN

Marks

Mark 1, c. 1930+

Mark 2, c. 1930+

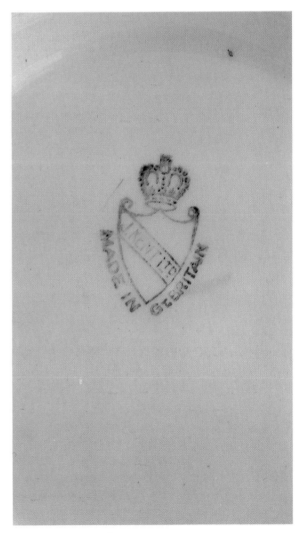

Mark 3, c. 1930+

Mark 5, c. 1930+

Mark 4, c. 1930+

Mark 6, c. 1955+

Mark 7, c. 1936-1939

Royal Brocade

Elijah Cotton Ltd.

NELSON POTTERY, HANLEY,
STOKE·ON·TRENT

Chapter 3
Lord Nelson

- 1889-1981
- Earthenware
- Hanley

Trade name used by Elijah Cotton Ltd., Nelson Pottery, Hanley.

In a November 1, 1929, Pottery Gazette ad, Nelson ware was proclaimed world famed for its high quality breakfast, tea and dinner ware, coffee, supper and fruit sets.

Previous Page: November 1947, Advertisement for *Royal Brocade* by Elijah Cotton, Ltd., Nelson Pottery, Hanley.

Patterns

Anemone, Vase, 5", $100-150.

Black Beauty, Cream, 2.25" high, Mark 1, $75-100.

Briar Rose, Cream, 2.25" high, Mark 1, $75-100.

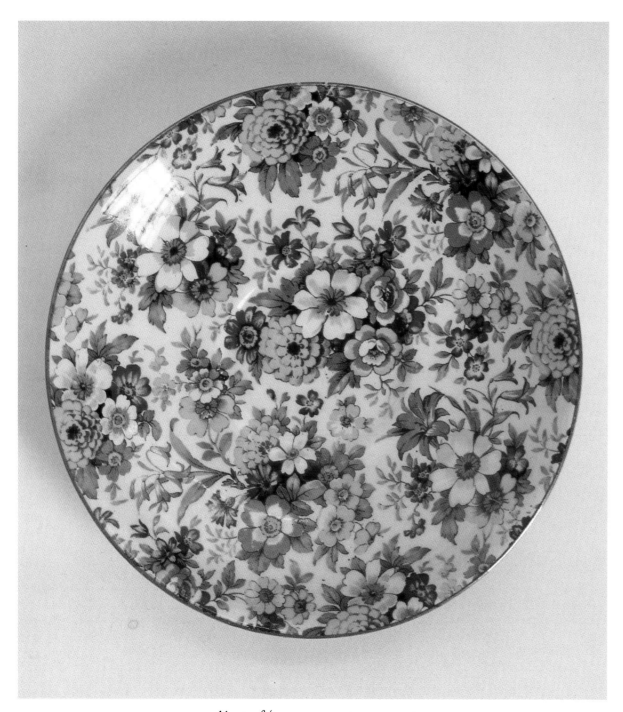

Marigold, Saucer, 5.75" diameter, Mark 1.

Country Lane, Plate, 4.75" diameter, Mark 2, $50-75.

Green Tulip, Plate, 5" diameter, Mark 2, $50-75.

Heather, Saucer, 5.75" diameter, Mark 1.

Marina, Plate, 6.5" diameter, Mark 1, $75-100.   *Marina* pattern close-up.

Skylark, Saucer, 5.75" diameter, Mark 1.

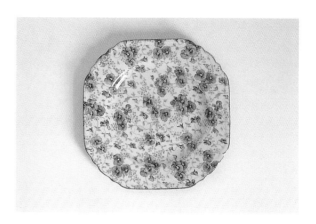

Pansy, Plate, 7.5" diameter, Mark 1, $75-100.

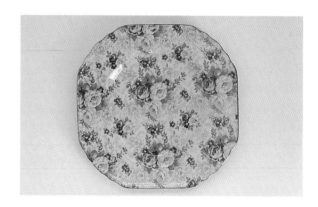

Rose Time, Plate, 6.5" diameter, Mark 1, $75-100.

Royal Brocade, Saucer, 5.75" diameter, Mark 1.

Shapes

Marina, Demi Cup, 2" high X 2" diameter, Mark 1.

Skylark, Demi Cup, 2" high X 2" diameter, Mark 1.

Marigold, Cup, 2.75" high X 3.25" diameter, Mark 1.

Skylark, Cup, 2.75" high X 3.25" diameter, Mark 1.

Skylark, Grandfather Cup and Saucer, 4" high X 4" diameter, Mark 1, $100-150.

Pansy, Vase, 5.25" high, Mark 1, $100-150.

Rose Time, Salt and Pepper, 2.75" High,
Mark 1, $75-125.

Rose Time, Egg Cup, 1.5" high X 1.75"
diameter, $50-75.

Rose Time, Jam Pot, 4" high X 3" diameter, Mark 1,
$100-150.

Rose Time, Sugar, 2.25" high X 3" diameter, and
Cream, 2.25" high X 3" diameter, Mark 1, $175-200.

Rose Time pattern close-up.

98 Chintz Ceramics

Black Beauty, Nut Dish, 6" X 3.5", Mark 1, $50-75.

Heather, Sugar, 2.25" high X 3" diameter, and Cream, 3" diameter, with Tray, 9.5" X 3", Mark 1, $200-225.

Marks

Mark 1, c. 1930+

Mark 2, c. 1930+

Chapter 4
Shelley

- 1872-1966
- China and Earthenware
- Longton

Began in 1872 as Wileman and Co. when Joseph Shelley and James Wileman became partners. In 1925, the company became known as Shelley Potteries, Ltd.

In 1966 Allied English Potteries acquired control of the Shelley Co. In 1971, Allied merged with the Doulton groups.

Previous Page: Former Shelley Factory Building, built in 1920. The building is the last of the Shelley Potteries, Ltd., Longton, Stoke-on-Trent. (Now owned by Royal Doulton.)

Pottery Gazette and Glass Trade Review, February 1948, advertising Shelley *Maytime*. Exported to Canada, Australia, New Zealand, South Africa, India, U.S.A.

Shelley Pattern Book, c. 1960, showing the variety of ways that *Summer Glory* chintz was applied.

Shelley Pattern Book, c. 1960, showing four chintz patterns (*Summer Glory, Melody, Blue Daisy, Green Daisy*).

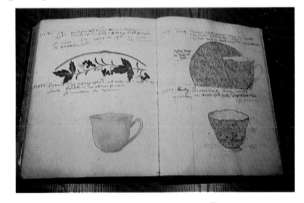

Shelly Pattern Book, c. 1960, showing *Primrose* chintz.

Shelly Pattern Book, c. 1960, showing four chintz patterns (*Maytime, Melody, Rock Garden, Summer Glory*).

Shelly Pattern Book, c. 1960, showing *Marguerite* chintz inside and outside cup.

Shelly Pattern Book, c. 1960, showing *Black Chintz* (very rare).

Patterns

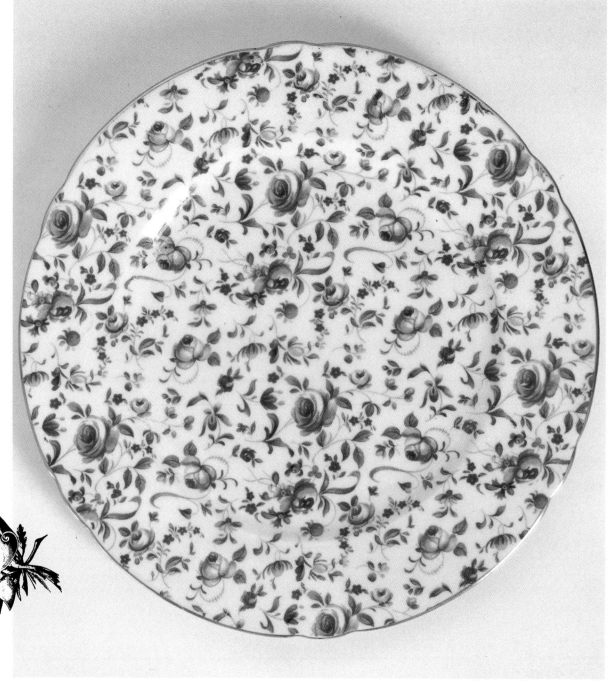

Briar Rose, Plate, 8", Mark 1, $75-100.

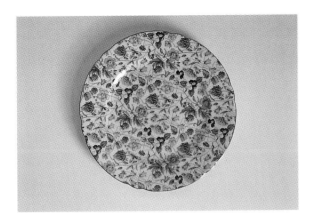

Countryside, Plate, 8", Mark 1, $100-125. Courtesy of H. DeConcini.

Marguerite, Mini Saucer, 3" diameter, Mark 1.

Maytime, Plate, 8", Mark 1, $100-125.

Melody, Plate, 8", Mark 1, $100-125.   *Melody* pattern close-up.

Pink Clover, Teapot (4 cup), Mark 1, $400-600.

Primrose, Cream, 4" high, Mark 1, $100-125.

Rock Garden, Saucer, 5.5", Mark 1.
Courtesy of C. Davenport.

Tapestry Rose, Sweet Dish, 5", Mark 1, $35-50.

Summer Glory, Plate, 8", Mark 3, $100-125. Courtesy of H. DeConcini.

Melody, Biscuit Barrel, 6" high X
7" diameter, Mark 2, Earthenware,
$300-500. (Very rare)

Melody, Cream, 3" high, and Sugar, 2" high, Mark 1, $200-250.

Melody, Posy holder, 2.5" high X 7" diameter, Mark 2, Earthenware, $300-400.

Melody, Cruet Set, 3" high, Mark 2, Earthenware, $250-300.

Maytime, Flower Ring, 1.5" high X 7" diameter, Mark 2, Earthenware, $150-200.

Maytime, Demitasse Cup, 2.5" high, Mark 1.

Melody, Cup, 3" high, Ripon Shape, Mark 1.

Melody, Cup, 2.5" high, Henley Shape, Mark 1.

Pink Clover, Cup, 2.5" high, Oleander Shape, Mark 1.
Courtesy of C. Davenport.

Melody, Apple Butter, 4" high, Mark 1, $100-150.

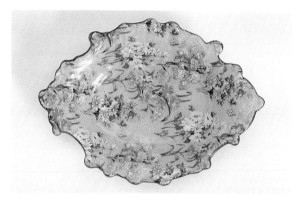

Melody, Sweet Dish, 7" X 4.5", Mark 1, $100-150.

Melody, Wall Pocket, 7.5" X 6", Mark 1, $500-700.
(Very rare)

Marks

Mark 1

Mark 2

Mark 3

All three of these marks date from c. 1925-1945.
The words Fine Bone China were added 1945-1966.

Chapter 5
Crown Ducal

• 1915-1967
• Earthenware
• Tunstall

Manufacturers of fine earthenware, dinner, tea, suite ware, and fancy goods. Trade name used by A.G. Richardson & Co., Ltd. Acquired by Enoch Wedgwood & Co., Ltd., Tunstall, Staffordshire Potteries.

"Crown Ducal—a brand of popular-priced earthenware which is generally recognized throughout the trade to possess attractions and merit."[1]

"Crown Ducal ware possesses the attributes of reliability and distinctiveness without being high priced and exclusive."[2]

Crown Ducal Ware was exported to U.S.A., Australia, New Zealand, South Africa, Argentine, Uruguay, and Switzerland.

[1] *Pottery Gazette & Glass Trade Review,* July 1932.
[2] _____.

Rose and Motifs Vase, 9" high, Mark 1, $300-400.

Octagon Bowl, 9" diameter X 4.25" high,
Mark 1, $200-300.

Ascot, Divided Plate, 11", Mark 2, $125-150.

Florida, Plate, 8", Mark 2, $75-100.

Blue Chintz, Plate, 6.5", Mark 2, $75-100.

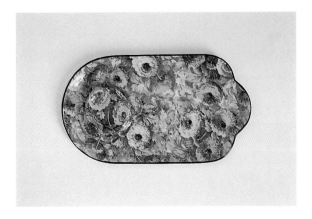

Marigold, Solitaire Tray, 9.5" X 5.5", Mark 2, $50-75.

Saucer, 5.5", Mark 2.

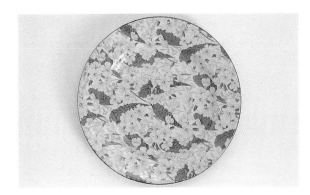

Primula, Plate, 7", Mark 3, $75-100.

Festival, Square Plate, 7.5", Mark 3, $75-100.

Peony, Square Plate, 7.5", Mark 3, $75-100.

Plate, 8", No Mark, $75-100.

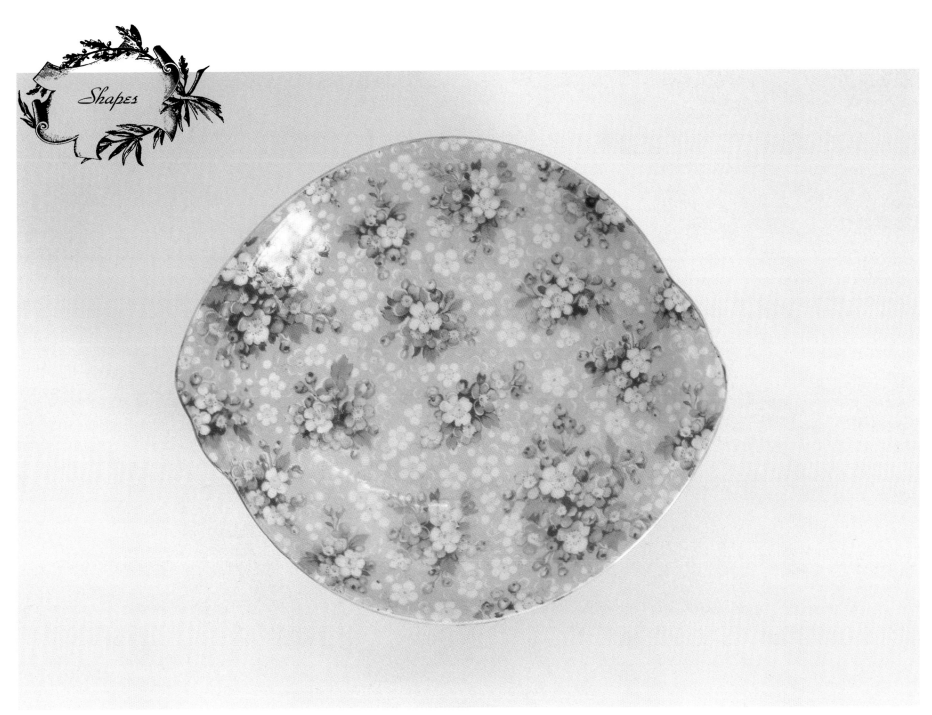

Priscilla, Comport, 6" diameter X 2.5" high, Mark 4, $50-75.

Teacup, 2.5" high, Mark 2.

Blue Chintz, Demitasse Cup, 2" high, Mark 2.

Ascot, Candlestick, 7" high, Mark 2, $150-200.

Ascot, Bowl, 9.5" diameter X 2.5" high, Mark 2, $150-200.

Ascot, Teacup, 2" high, Mark 2.

Primula, Teacup, 2.75" high, Mark 3.

Ascot, Vase, 14" high, Mark 2, $250-350.

Priscilla, Mint Sauce, 3" high, Mark 4, $55-75.

Ascot, Saucer, 5.5" diameter, Mark 2.

Ascot, Vases, 8" high, Mark 2, $200-250 ea.

Mark 1, c. 1916+

Mark 3, c. 1925+

Mark 2, c. 1930+

Mark 4, c. 1925+

Chapter 6
Empire

- 1896-1967
- Earthenware
- Stoke

Trade name Empire Porcelain Co., Ltd.

Patterns

Previous Page:
Lilac Time, Plate, 7", Mark 1, $75-100.

Maytime, Double Egg Cup, Mark 2, $50-75.

Maytime, Plate, 6.5", Mark 2, $75-100.

Maytime, Sweet Dish, Mark 2, $50-75.

Water Lily, Plate, 8", Mark 1, $75-100.

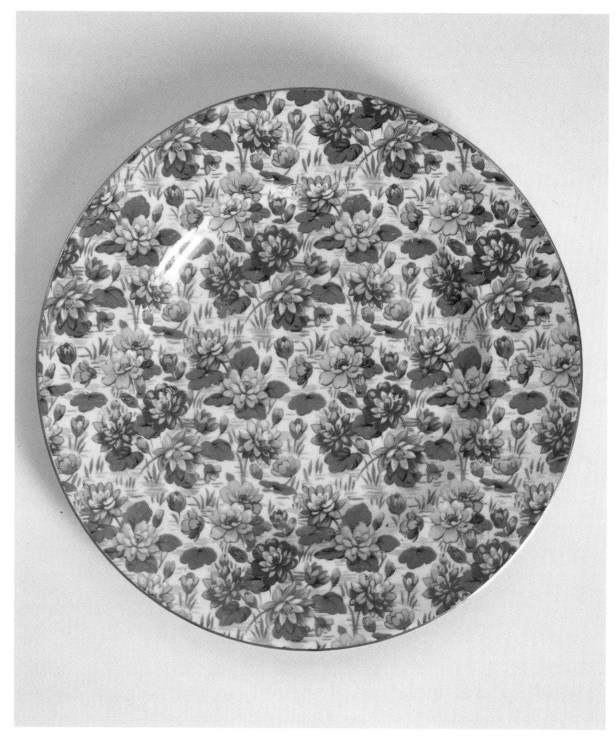

Shapes

Lilac Time, Demitasse Cup and Saucer, 3" high, Mark 1, $100-150.

Lilac Time, Open Sugar, 2" high X 3.5" diameter, and Cream, 2.5" high, Mark 1, $200-250.

Lilac Time, Teapot (4 cup), 8" high, Mark 1, $400-600.

Lilac Time, Open Sugar, 1.75" high X 3" diameter, and Cream, 2.75" high, Mark 1, $200-250.

Lilac Time, Ashtray, 4" X 4", Mark 1, $50-75.

Marks

Mark 1, c. 1930s

Mark 2, c. 1930s

Lilac Time, Comport by Empire, 10" w, 5" h. $50-100.

Chapter 7
Other English Chintz
Rosina China Co. Ltd.

- 1941-Present
- China
- Longton

Patterns
(unnamed)

Saucer, 5.5", Mark 1.

Saucer, 5.5", Mark 1.

Saucer, 5.5", Mark 1.

"Briar Rose,"
Saucer, 5.5", Mark 1.

"Tapestry," Teacup, 3" high, Mark 1.

Shapes

Cigarette Box, 5" X 4", and 2 Ashtrays, 3" X 2", Mark 1, $200-250. (Very rare)

Teacup, 2.5" high, Mark 1.

"Briar Rose," Mini Cup and Saucer, 1" high, $100-150.

Teacup, 2.5" high, Mark 1.

W.R. Midwinter Ltd.

- 1910-Present
- Earthenware
- Burslem

Established in 1910 by W.R. Midwinter at Bournes Park Pottery, Burslem.

W.R. Midwinter, Ltd., Advertisement, March 1949, *Springtime Chintz*, "Pottery Gazette and Glass Trade Review."

W.R. Midwinter, Ltd., Advertisement, May 1947, *Springtime Chintz*, "Pottery Gazette and Glass Trade Review."

Springtime Chintz, Demitasse Cup, 2" high, Mark 2.

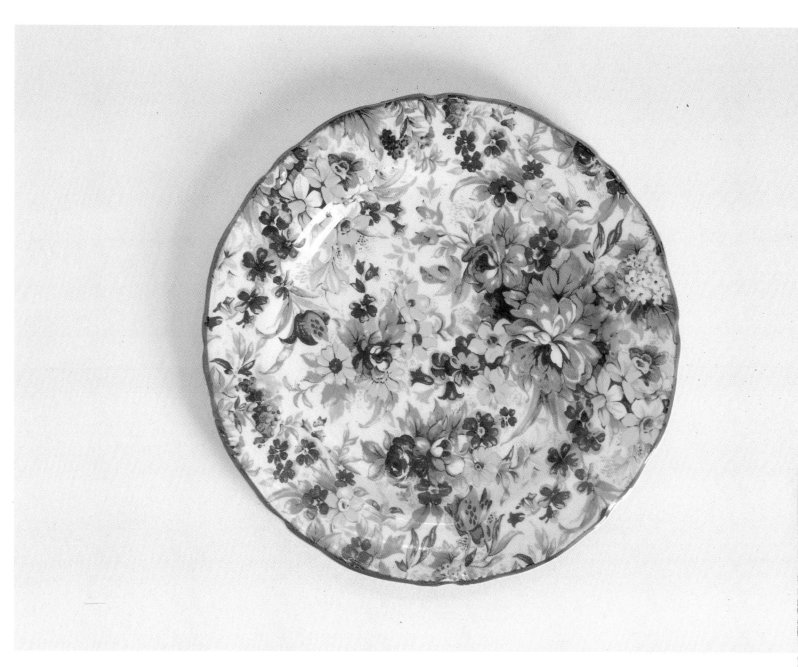

Springtime Chintz, Plate, 6", Mark 1, $75-100.

Springtime Chintz
pattern close-up.

No Pattern Name, Plate, 9", Midwinter, $75-100.

Arthur J. Wilkinson, Ltd.

- •1885-1964
- •Earthenware and Ironstone
- •Burslem

A. J. Wilkinson, Ltd., Advertisement, May 1949, *Lorna Doone*. (Exported to South Africa, Canada, New York, Cuba, Australia, New Zealand, Holland, Belgium, Norway, Argentine.)

Lorna Doone, Bowl, 5.5" diameter, $55-75.

Lorna Doone, Dresser Set, $200-300.

Sadler & Sons (Ltd.)

- 1882-Present
- Earthenware
- Burslem

Sadler and Sons has been primarily a teapot manufacturer.

Sadler, Jug, 5" high, Mark 3, $100-125.

Barker Bros., Ltd.

- 1876-1978
- China and Earthenware
- Meir Works, Longton

Part of Alfred Clough group in 1959. Then in 1978 became Grindley of Stoke (Ceramics) Ltd.

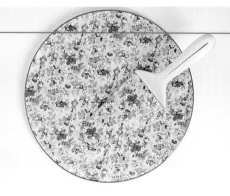

Cake Plate, 11", and Server, Royal Tudor Ware, Barker Bros., Mark 4, $150-200.

Cream, 3" high, Tudor Ware, Barker Bros., Mark 5, $55-75.

Cake Plate, 11", and Server, Royal Tudor Ware, Barker Bros., Mark 4, $150-200.

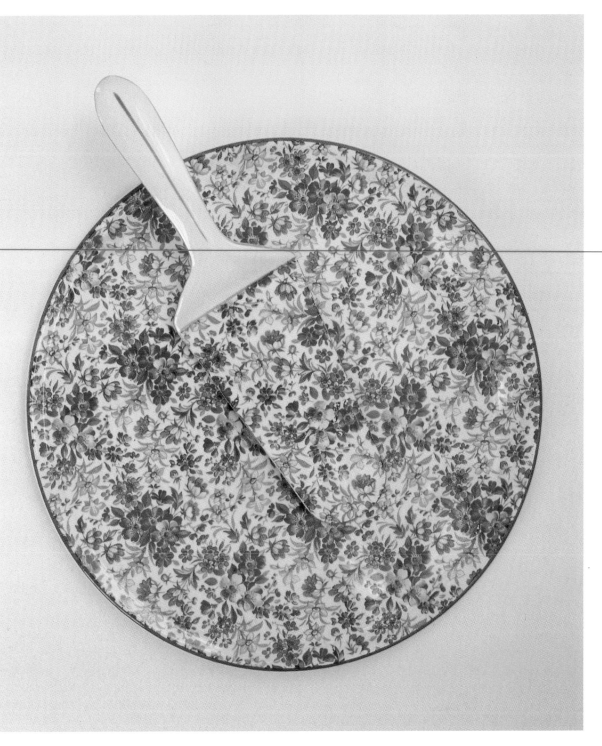

Wade, Heath & Co. (Ltd.)

- 1927-Present
- Earthenware
- Burslem

Part of the Wade Group of Potters or Wade Ceramics, Ltd.

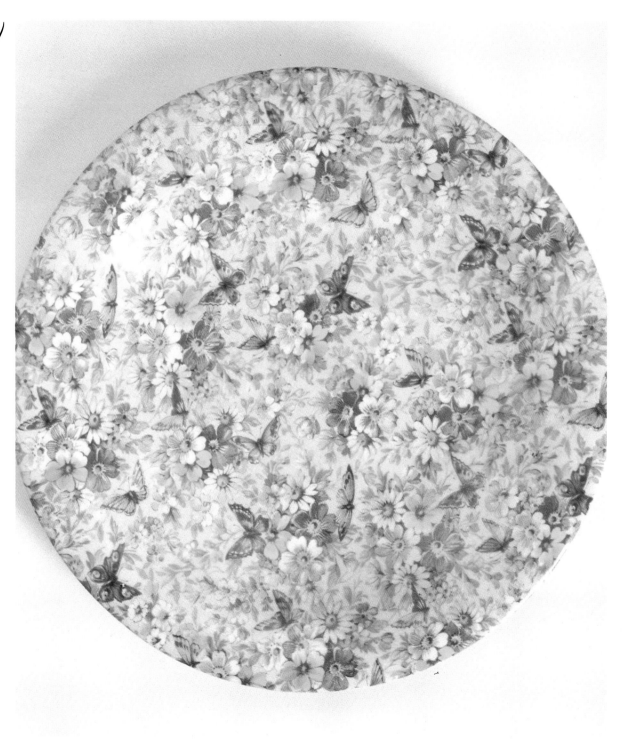

Chintz Floral and Butterfly, Plate, 9",
Pattern L-4810, Wade Heath, Mark 6, $75-100.

Ridgway Ltd.

- 1910-1952
- Earthenware
- Shelton

Taken over by Royal Doulton. Ridgway (Bedford Works) was built at Shelton in 1866 by Edward John Ridgway, who belonged to a family of famous potters.

Unnamed Ridgway pattern close-up.

Bowl, 5" diameter, Ridgway, Mark 7, $75-100.

Hollinshead & Kirkham, Ltd.

- •1870-1956
- •Earthenware
- •Tunstall

Factory purchased by Johnson Bros., Ltd., in 1956.

"*Pansy,*" Teapot (4 cup), 6" high, H&K, Mark 8, $400-600.

Sampson Smith, Ltd.

- 1846-1963
- Earthenware and china
- Longton

"*Pansy,*" Cup, 3" high, Sampson Smith, Mark 9.

Plate, 6 1/2", No Mark, $75-100.

Double Egg Cup, 3 1/2" high, No Mark, $55-75.

"Pansy," Vases, 14" high, No Mark, $200-250 each.

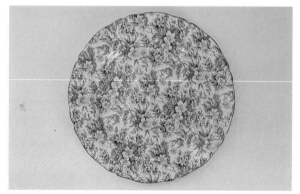

Plate, 10", No Mark, $75-100.

Crown Clarence

- 1922-1946
- Earthenware
- Longton

Trade name used by Operative Wholesale Society, Ltd.

"*Briar Rose*," Salt Shaker, 2.5" high, Crown Clarence, Mark 10, $55-75.

Also producing chintz:
Colclough China, Ltd.

- 1937-1948
- China
- Longton
Taken over by Royal Doulton.

Kensington Pottery

- 1922-1937
- Earthenware
- Hanley

John Shaw & Sons, Ltd.

- 1931-1963
- China and Earthenware
- Longton

Adderlys, Ltd.

- 1905-1947
- China and Earthenware
- Longton
Taken over by Ridgway Potteries, Ltd., in 1947.

Thomas Hughes & Son, Ltd.

- 1895-1957
- China and Earthenware
- Burslem
Taken over by Arthur Wood & Sons, 1961.

Mark 2., no date

Mark 1A., c. 1952+

Mark 3., c. 1947+

Mark 1B., c. 1932-41

Mark 4., c. 1937+

Mark 5., c. 1937

Mark 6., c. 1939+

Mark 7., c. 1950+

Mark 8.,
c. 1933-42

Mark 9.,
c. 1940s

Mark 10.,
c. 1950+

Chapter 8
E.R. Phila

- 1886-Present
- Porcelain

Ebeling and Ruess is an importing company based in Philadelphia. Following WWI porcelain items were imported from Czechoslovakia and sold in America.

Previous Page:
Cheery Chintz, Saucer, 5.5", Mark 2.

Patterns

Chelsea, Tray, 8" X 5", Mark 1, $50-75.

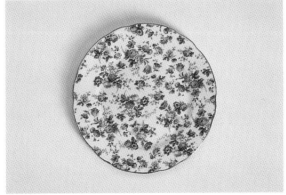

Dorset—Cheery Chintz, Plate, 8", Mark 3, $40-50.

Portland, Plate, 8", Mark 3, $40-50.

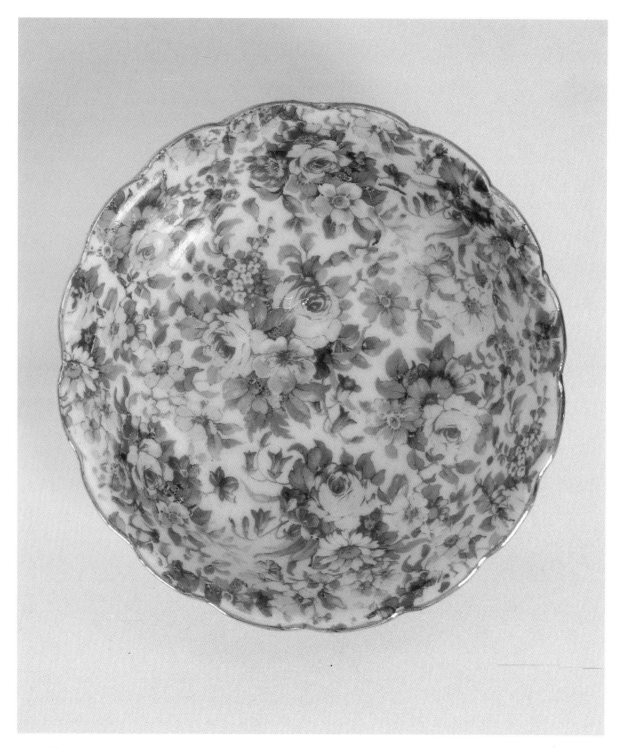

Sussex—Cheery Chintz, Plate, 12",
Mark 2, $100-150.

Warwick, Plate, 5.5", Mark 4, $40-50.

Stratford, Bowl, 5.5", Mark 3, $40-50.

Portland, Divided Dish, 7" X 5", Mark 3, $40-50.

Shapes

Marks

Mark 2

Cheery Chintz, Teacup, 2.25" high, Mark 2.

Warwick, Vase, 7" high,
Mark 4, $75-125.

Mark 1

Mark 3

Sussex—Cheery Chintz, Plate 11",
Mark 2, $100-150.

Mark 4

Japanese Chintz

Copies of popular English chintz patterns were hand painted by the Japanese and imported to America. The pieces were primarily sold in five-and-dime stores.

"*Welbeck,*" Salt, 2.5" high, with Tray, 6" X 2", Mark 1, $20-50.

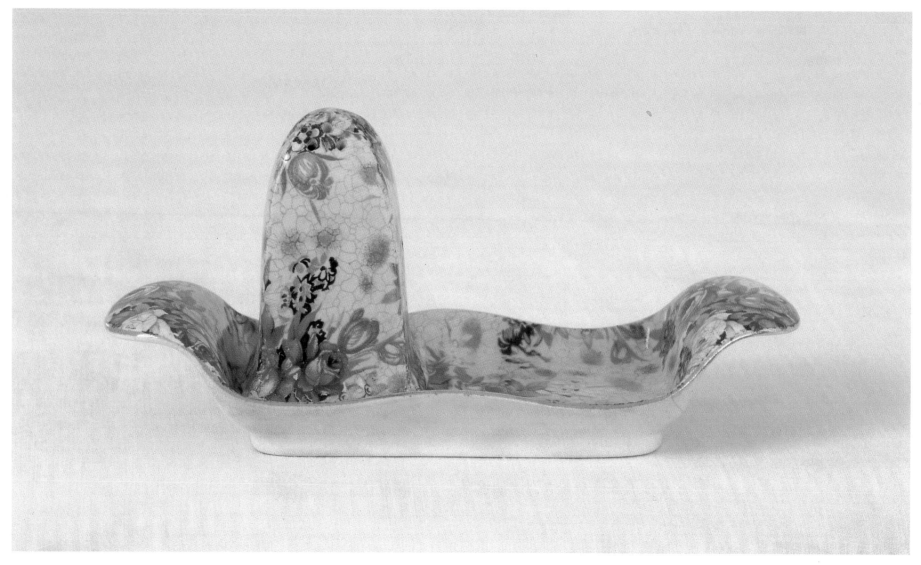

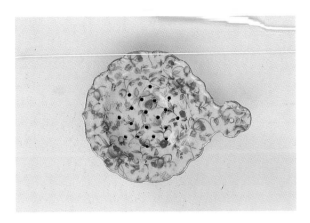

"Briar Rose," Tea Strainer, 5" X 3.5", No Mark, $25-35.

"Beeston," Trefoil, 8", Mark 2, $50-75.

"Old Cottage," Ashtray, 5", Mark 3, $25-35.

"Summertime," Divided Dish, 6" X 6", Mark 4, $25-35.

"Julia," Stacking teapot, 1997. First piece of Chintz to be made in over 30 years. Limited edition of 1000. $350.
Contact The Chintz Connection (page 156) for details.

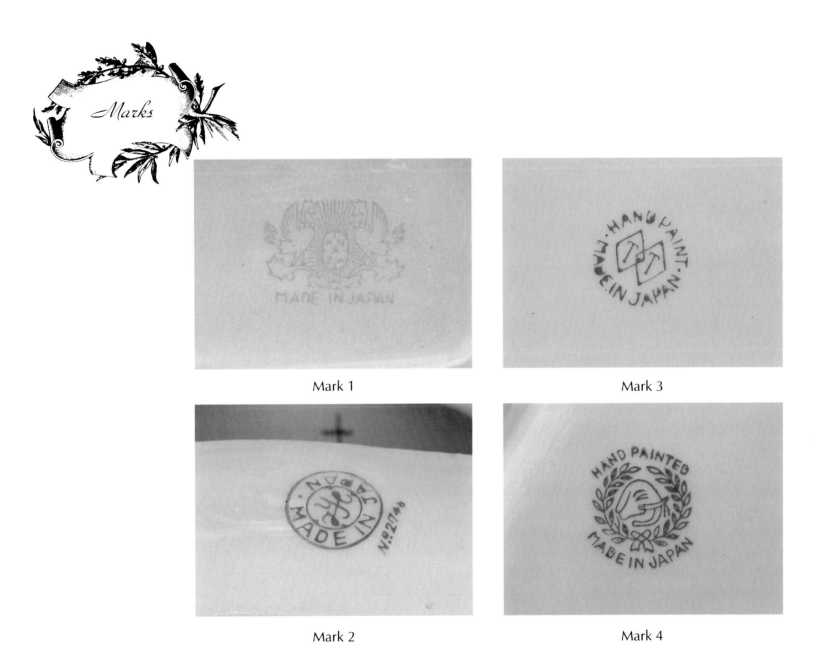

Mark 1

Mark 3

Mark 2

Mark 4

Collector's Notes

Chintz jewelry is an ideal solution for salvaging broken chintz. Custom-made chintz jewelry designed with silver mountings, available from THE CHINTZ CONNECTION, THE CHINTZ DATABASE. The Connection and Database will help you buy, sell, or trade English Chintz. For more information on the jewelry and the database, send an SASE to: The Chintz Connection, P.O. Box 222, Riverdale, MD 20738.

Value Reference

The value references in the captions reflect the average price of chintz found in the USA, United Kingdom, and Canada. The author assumes no liability for any losses occurred from using these references.

Epilogue

It is often said that the hunt is just as exciting as finding the object of desire. So if you have found patterns that have not been included in this book or shapes that have not been mentioned, please let me hear from you.
Happy Chintzing!

Bibliography

The Burlington Magazine for Connoisseurs, Volume 6, October 1904 to March/ 1905.

The Burlington Magazine, Ltd., London, pp. 232-234.

Ceramics, Arrow Press Publication, London: The Sidney Press, Ltd.

Godden, Geoffrey A. *Encyclopedia of British Pottery and Porcelain Marks,* 1964, London: Herbert Jenkins, Ltd.

Miller, Muriel. Article in *Antique Collecting,* Vol. 27, No. 2, June 1992, pp. 29-33.

Pottery and Glass, Founded 1918, and *Pottery and Glass Record,* London: Stratford Press, Ltd.

Pottery Gazette & Glass Trade Review, Est. 1875, London: Scott Greenwood & Son, Ltd., Proprietors.

Watkins, Chris, William Harvey, and Robert Senft. *Shelley Potteries: The History and Production of a Staffordshire Family of Potters,* 1980, London: Barrie & Jenkins.

Index